Easy Christmas Origami

John Montroll

Dover Publications, Inc., Mineola, New York

Bibliographical Note

Easy Christmas Origami is a new work, first published by
Dover Publications, Inc., in 2006.

International Standard Book Number

ISBN-13: 978-0-486-45024-7
ISBN-10: 0-486-45024-4

Manufactured in the United States by Courier Corporation
45024404
www.doverpublications.com

Introduction

"Deck the halls with boughs of holly . . . ." Decorate your Christmas Tree and house with fun, easy origami ornaments. You can put a star or angel on top of the tree, hang candy canes from branches, and even fold a stocking to hang by the fireplace. Here are 30 simple-to-fold models that will provide hours of holiday fun. You will also find a snowman, candle, and even Santa Claus himself in this joyful collection of Christmas origami.

The diagrams are drawn in the international Randlett-Yoshizawa style which is easy to follow once you have learned the basic folds. Origami paper is colored on one side and white on the other. In the diagrams, the shading represents the colored side. Origami paper can be found in many hobby shops or purchased by mail from OrigamiUSA, 15 West 77th Street, New York, NY 10024-5192 or from Dover Publications, Inc., 31 East 2nd Street, Mineola, NY 11501. Large sheets are easier to use than small ones.

I want to thank Gay Merrill Gross for her models, the Gift Box and 3D Tree, and Linda Mihara for her Santa Claus design.

Contents

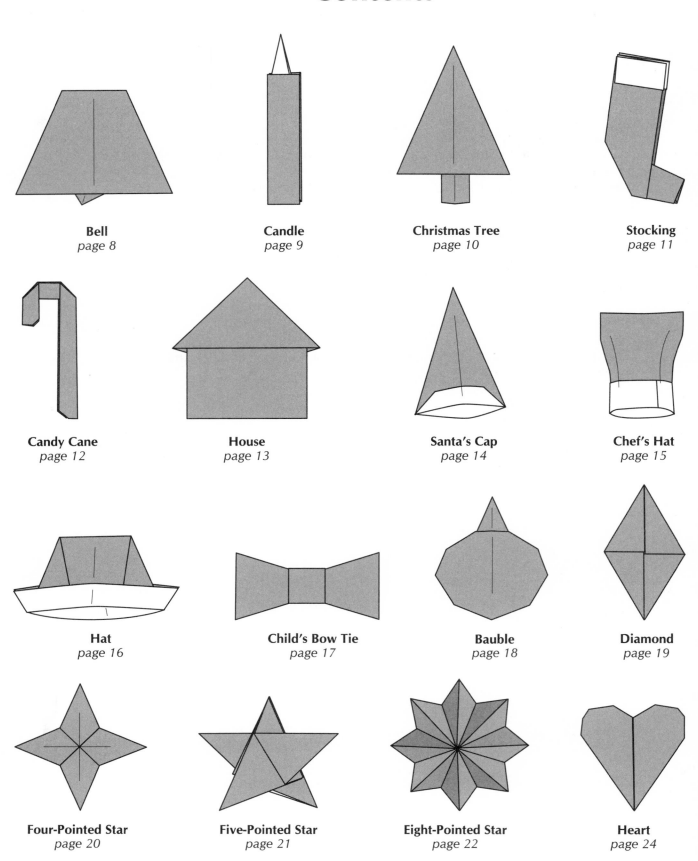

Bell
page 8

Candle
page 9

Christmas Tree
page 10

Stocking
page 11

Candy Cane
page 12

House
page 13

Santa's Cap
page 14

Chef's Hat
page 15

Hat
page 16

Child's Bow Tie
page 17

Bauble
page 18

Diamond
page 19

Four-Pointed Star
page 20

Five-Pointed Star
page 21

Eight-Pointed Star
page 22

Heart
page 24

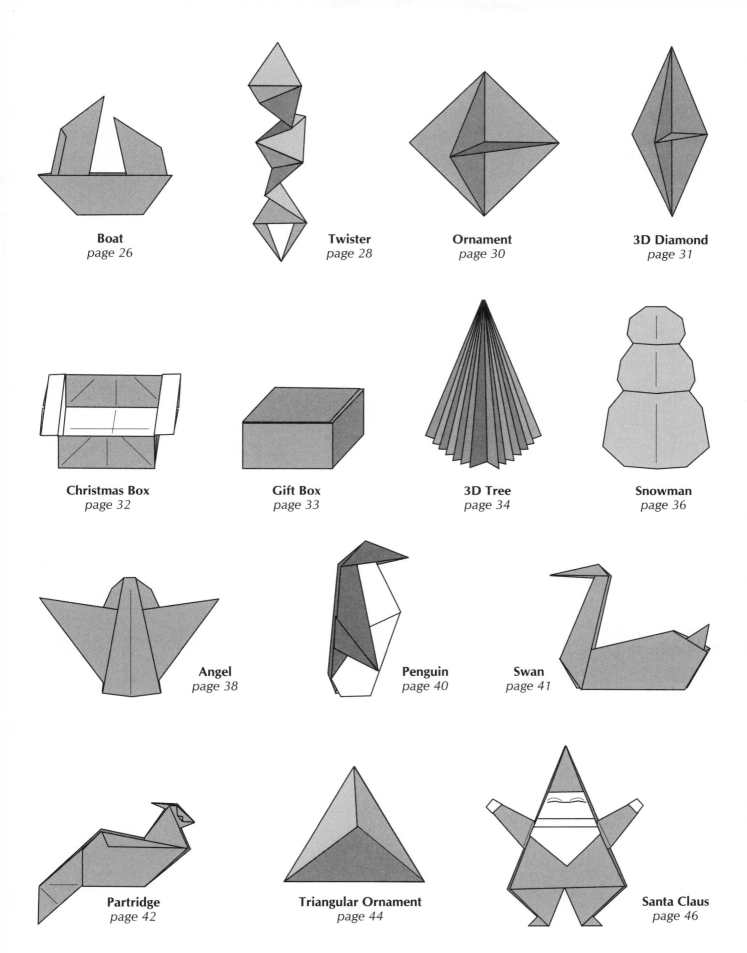

Boat
page 26

Twister
page 28

Ornament
page 30

3D Diamond
page 31

Christmas Box
page 32

Gift Box
page 33

3D Tree
page 34

Snowman
page 36

Angel
page 38

Penguin
page 40

Swan
page 41

Partridge
page 42

Triangular Ornament
page 44

Santa Claus
page 46

Symbols

Lines

- - - - - - - - - -   Valley fold, fold in front.

- - ·· - ·· - ·· - ·· - ·· -   Mountain fold, fold behind.

————————   Crease line.

··························   X-ray or guide line.

Arrows

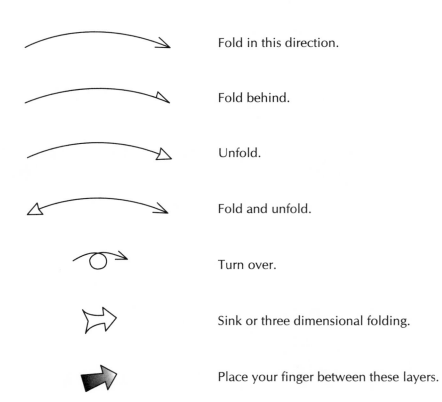

Fold in this direction.

Fold behind.

Unfold.

Fold and unfold.

Turn over.

Sink or three dimensional folding.

Place your finger between these layers.

Bell

1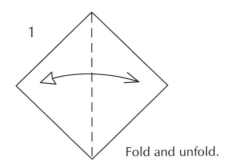

Fold and unfold.

2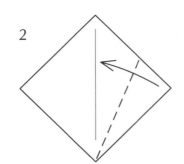

3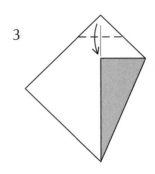

4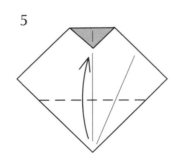

Unfold.

5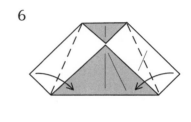

6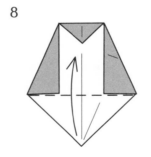

7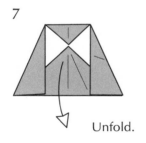

Unfold.

8

9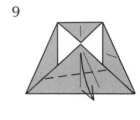

10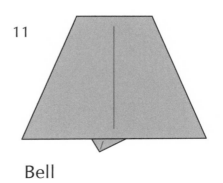

11

Bell

Candle

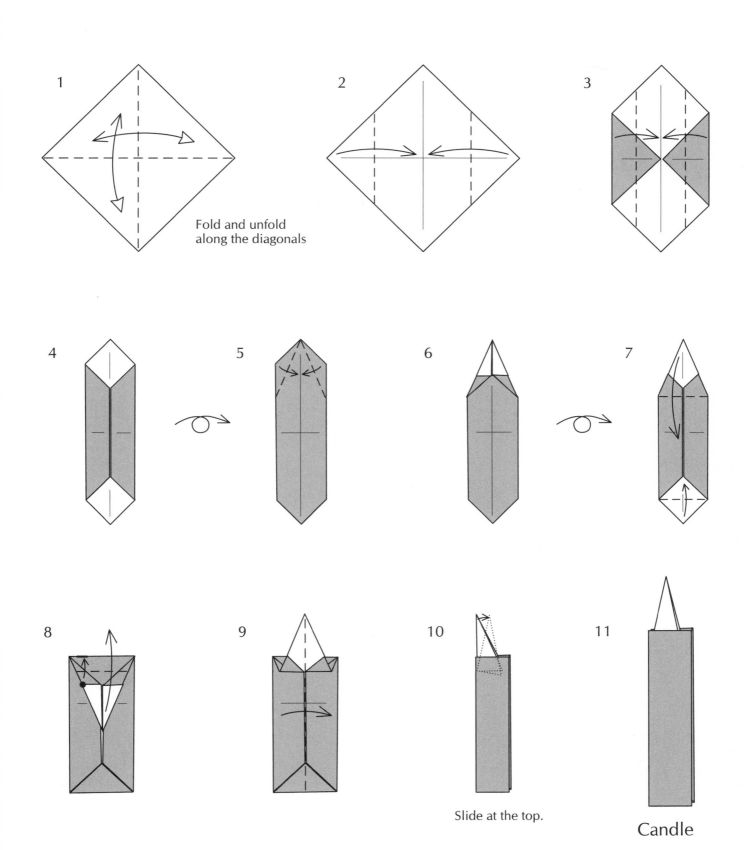

1

Fold and unfold
along the diagonals

2

3

4

5

6

7

8

9

10

Slide at the top.

11

Candle

Christmas Tree

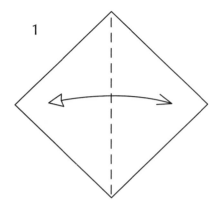

1

Fold and unfold.

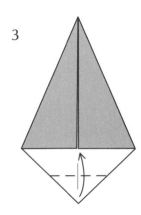

2

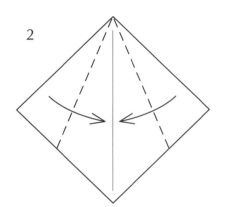

3

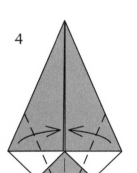

4

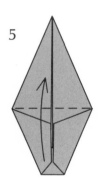

5

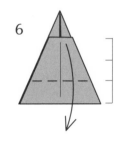

6

Fold down approximately
one third.

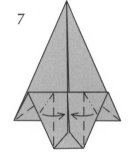

7

Fold towards the center.

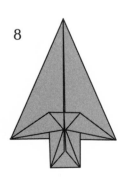

8

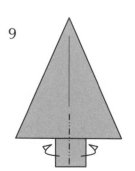

9

Bend slightly so the
tree can stand.

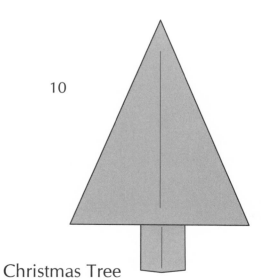

10

Christmas Tree

Stocking

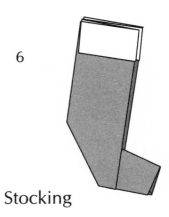

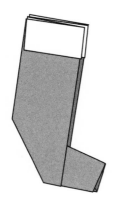

1

Fold a strip down. The size can vary.

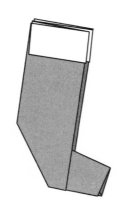

2

3

Repeat behind.

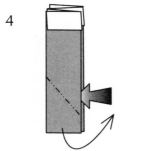

4

Fold between the layers.
The location can vary.

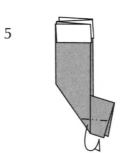

5

Fold inside.
Repeat behind.

6

Stocking

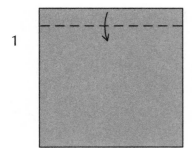

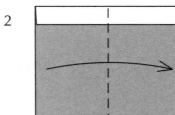

Candy Cane

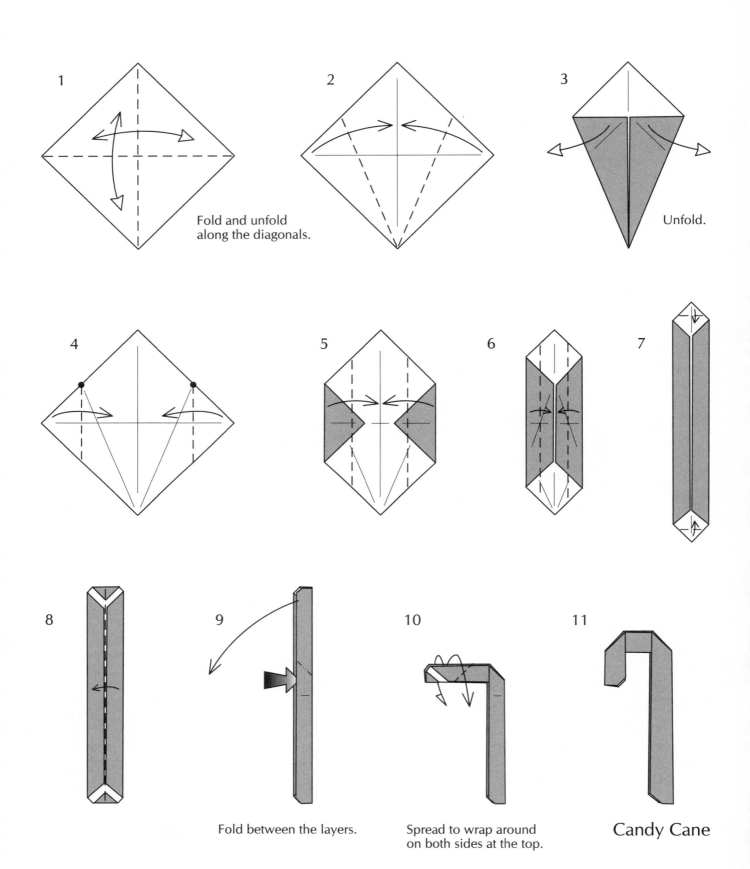

1 Fold and unfold along the diagonals.

2

3 Unfold.

4

5

6

7

8

9 Fold between the layers.

10 Spread to wrap around on both sides at the top.

11 Candy Cane

House

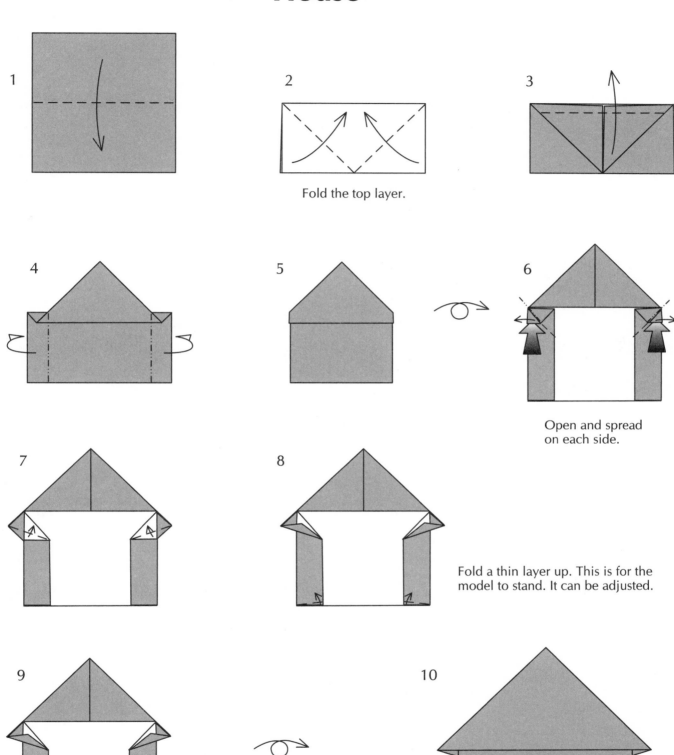

1

2

Fold the top layer.

3

4

5

6

Open and spread on each side.

7

8

Fold a thin layer up. This is for the model to stand. It can be adjusted.

9

Spread a little so the model can stand.

10

House

Santa's Cap

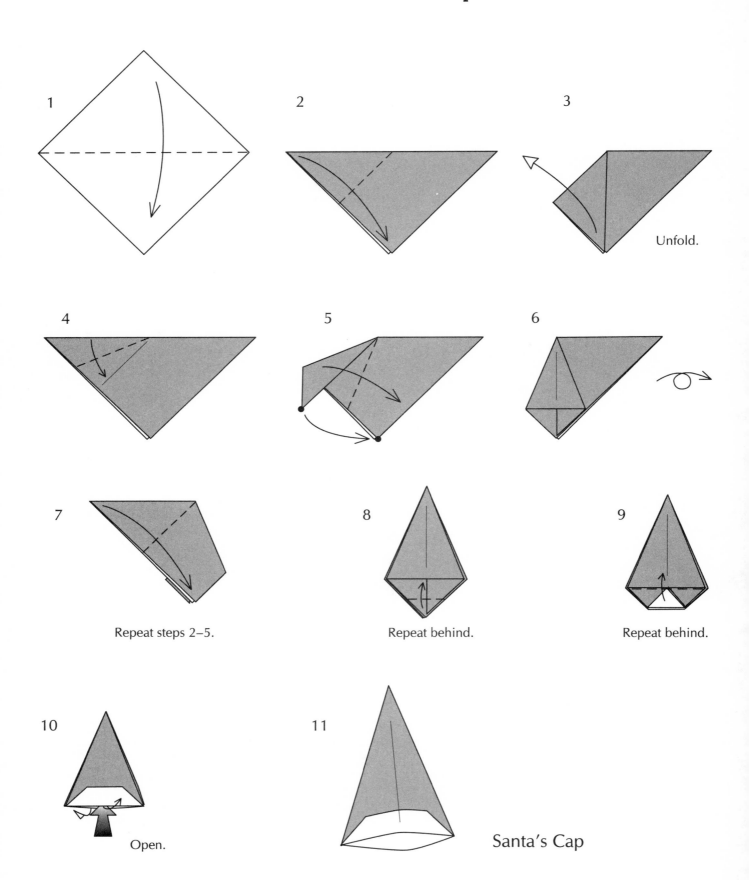

1

2

3

Unfold.

4

5

6

7

Repeat steps 2–5.

8

Repeat behind.

9

Repeat behind.

10

Open.

11

Santa's Cap

Chef's Hat

1

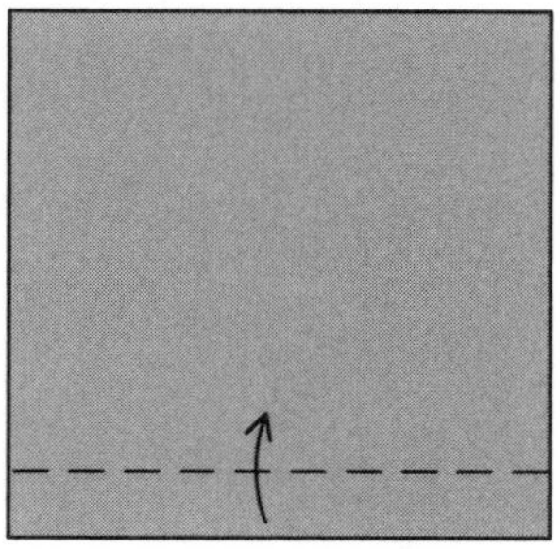

Fold a strip up. The size can vary.

2

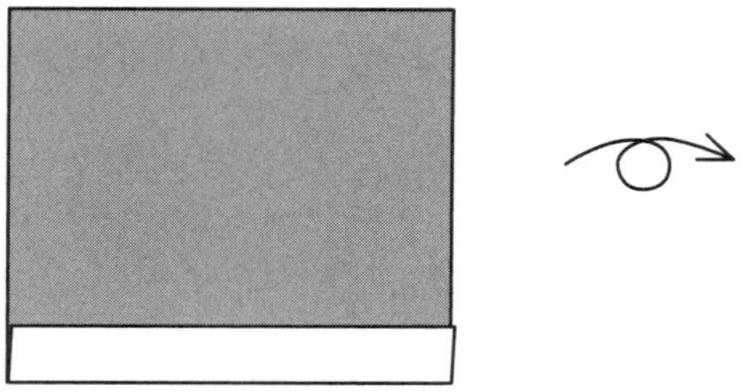

3

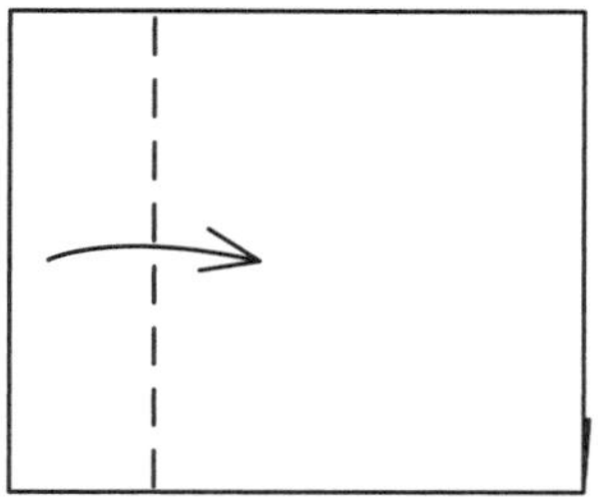

Fold to the right.
The size can vary.

4

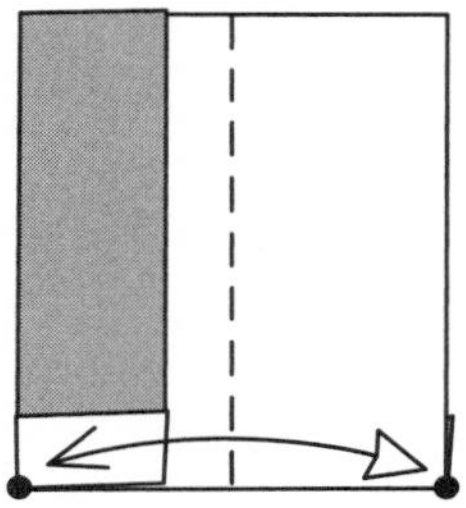

Fold and unfold.

5

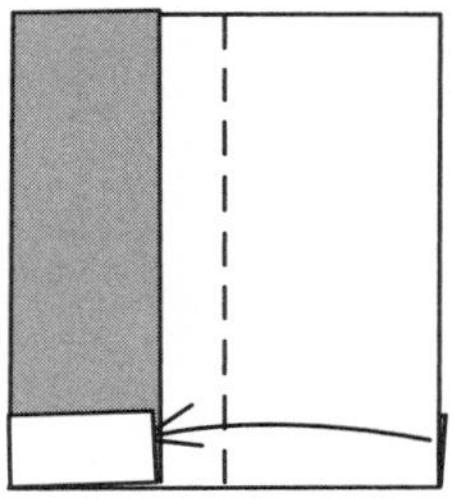

Tuck inside.

6

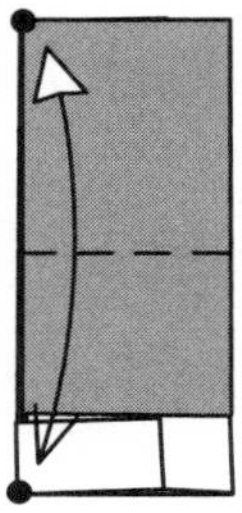

Fold and unfold.

7

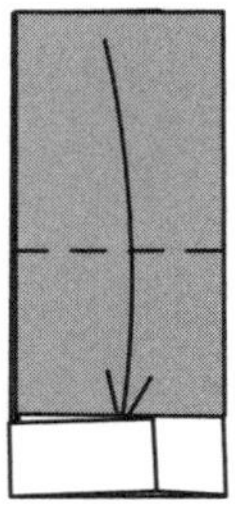

Tuck inside.

8

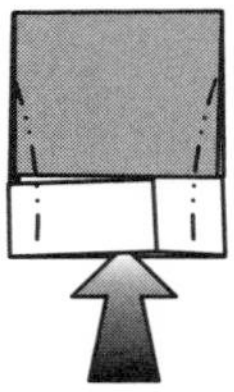

Open.

9

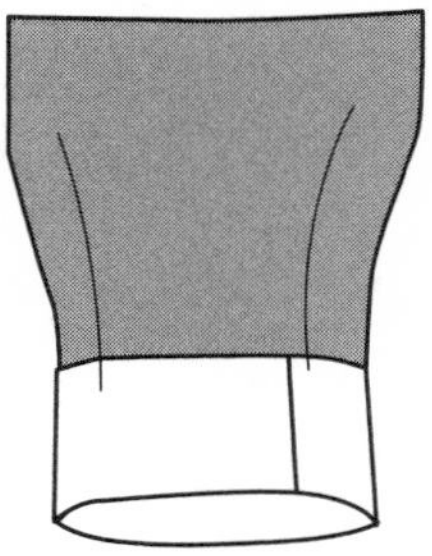

Chef's Hat

Hat

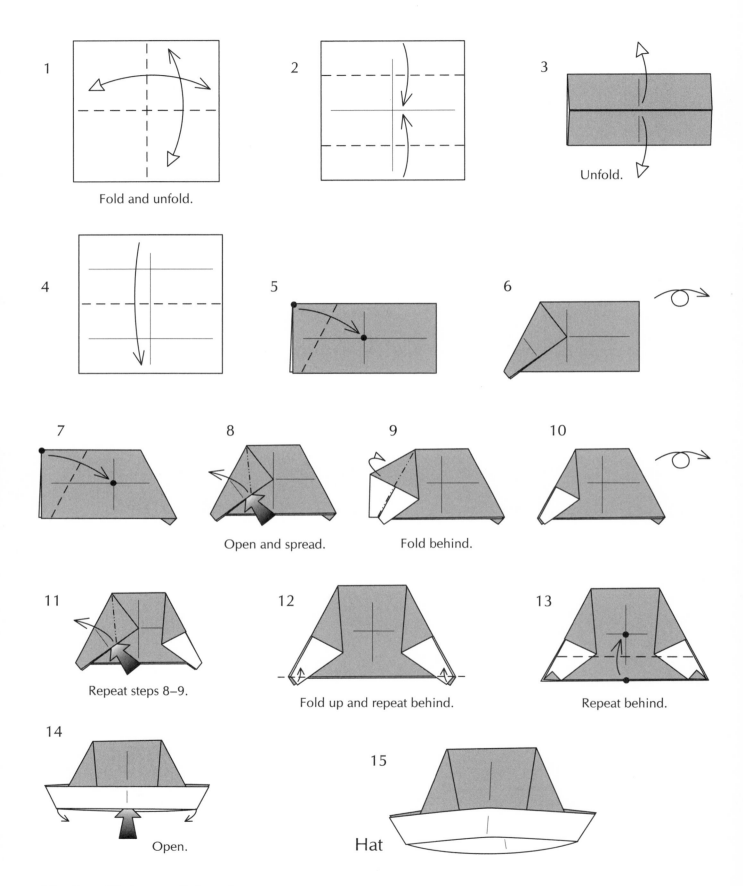

1 Fold and unfold.

2

3 Unfold.

4

5

6

7

8 Open and spread.

9 Fold behind.

10

11 Repeat steps 8–9.

12 Fold up and repeat behind.

13 Repeat behind.

14 Open.

15 Hat

Child's Bow Tie

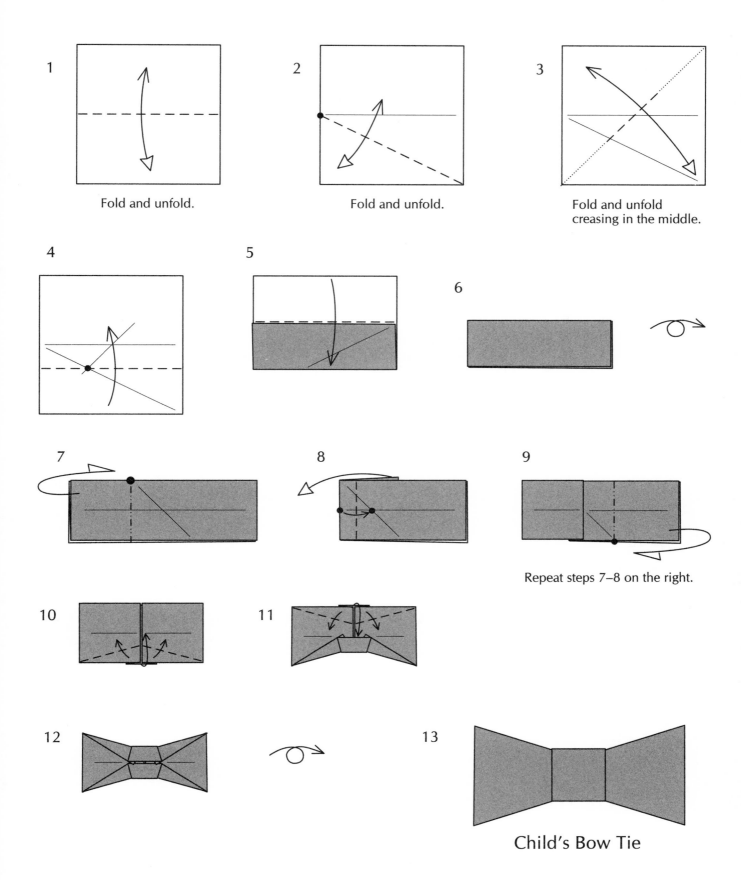

1 Fold and unfold.

2 Fold and unfold.

3 Fold and unfold creasing in the middle.

4

5

6

7

8

9 Repeat steps 7–8 on the right.

10

11

12

13 Child's Bow Tie

Bauble

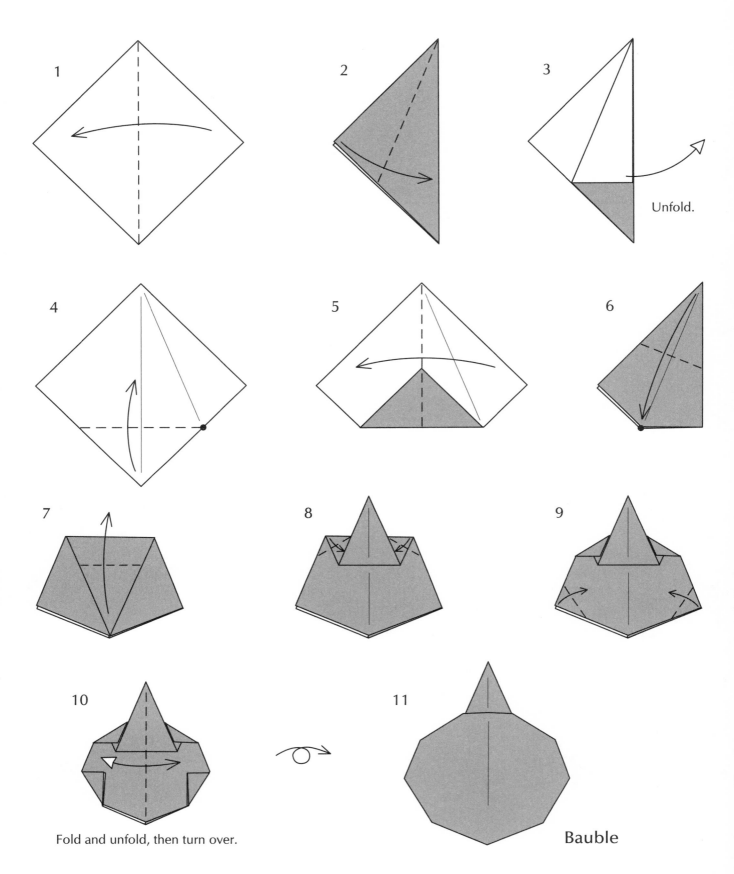

1

2

3

Unfold.

4

5

6

7

8

9

10

Fold and unfold, then turn over.

11

Bauble

Diamond

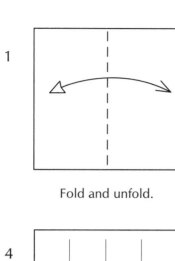

1 Fold and unfold.

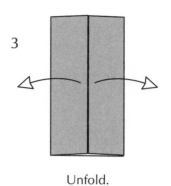

2

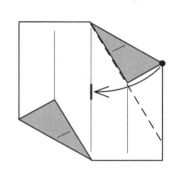

3 Unfold.

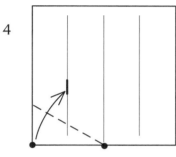

4 Fold the left corner to the crease.

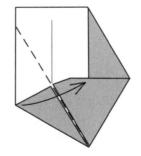

5 Fold the right corner to the crease.

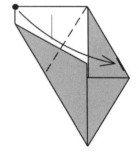

6 Bring the dot to the center line.

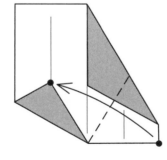

7

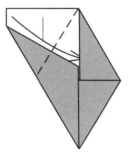

8

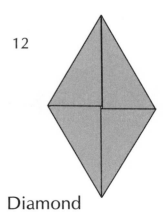

9

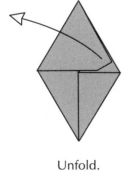

10 Unfold.

11 Tuck inside.

12

Diamond

Four-Pointed Star

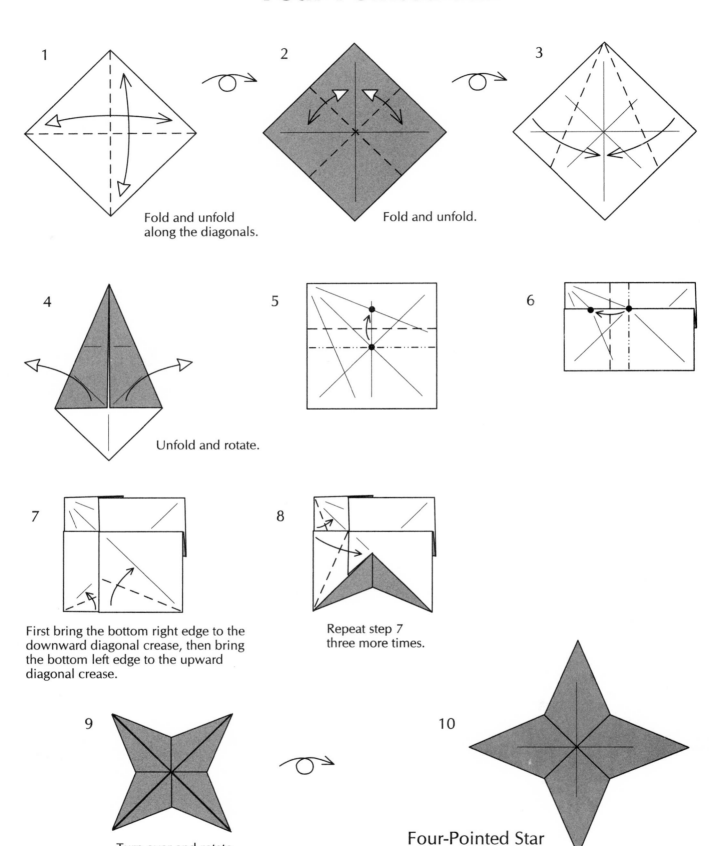

1

Fold and unfold along the diagonals.

2

Fold and unfold.

3

4

Unfold and rotate.

5

6

7

First bring the bottom right edge to the downward diagonal crease, then bring the bottom left edge to the upward diagonal crease.

8

Repeat step 7 three more times.

9

Turn over and rotate.

10

Four-Pointed Star

Five-Pointed Star

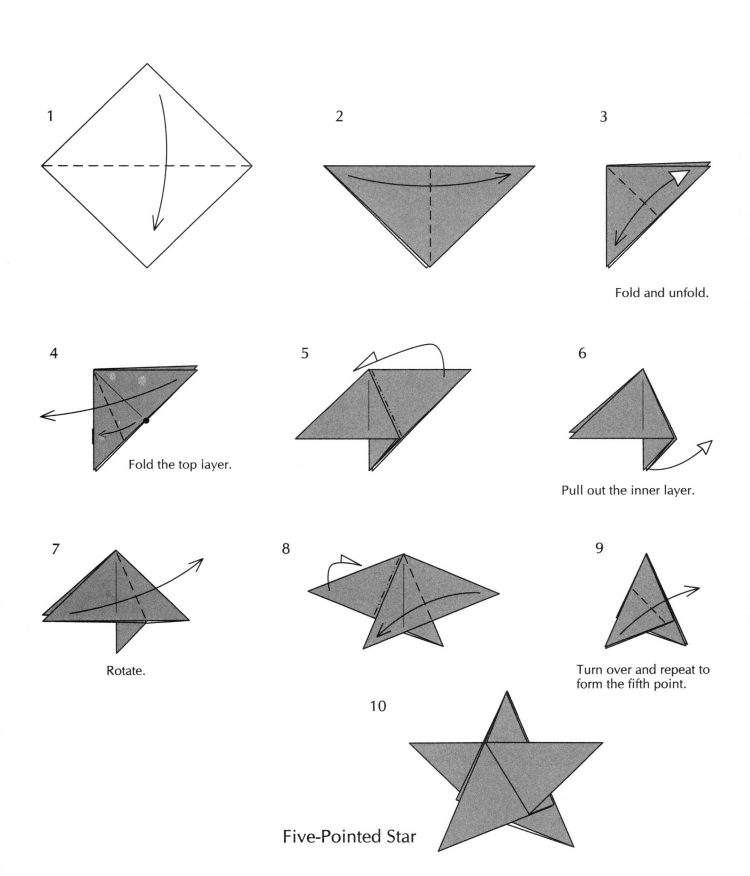

1

2

3

Fold and unfold.

4

Fold the top layer.

5

6

Pull out the inner layer.

7

Rotate.

8

9

Turn over and repeat to form the fifth point.

10

Five-Pointed Star

Eight-Pointed Star

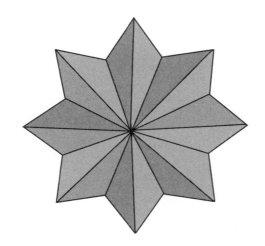

1

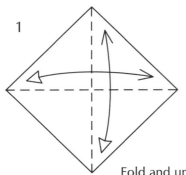

Fold and unfold
along the diagonals.

2

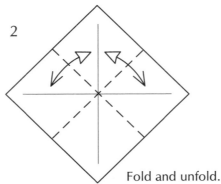

Fold and unfold.

3

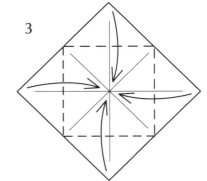

4

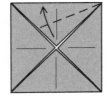

5

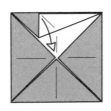

Unfold.

6

Fold and unfold.

7

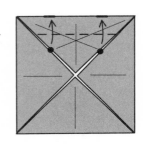

8

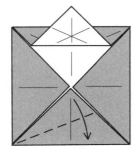

Repeat steps 4–7
at the bottom.

9

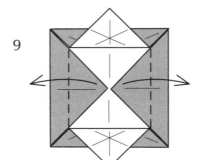

10

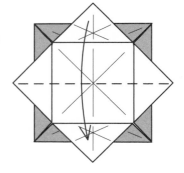

11

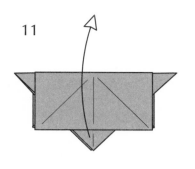

Unfold.

12

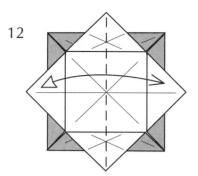

Fold and unfold.

13

14

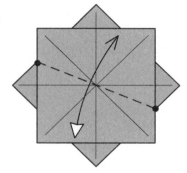

Fold and unfold.

15

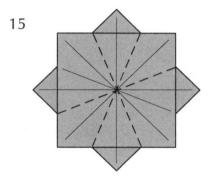

Fold and unfold
three more times.

16

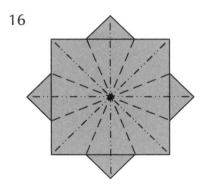

Fold along the creases and puff
out at the dot in the center. The
model will be three-dimensional.

17

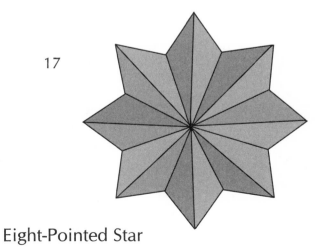

Eight-Pointed Star

Heart

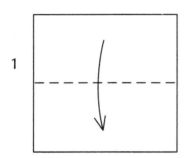

1

2

Fold and unfold.

3

Fold the top layer.

4

Unfold.

5

Fold both layers together.

6

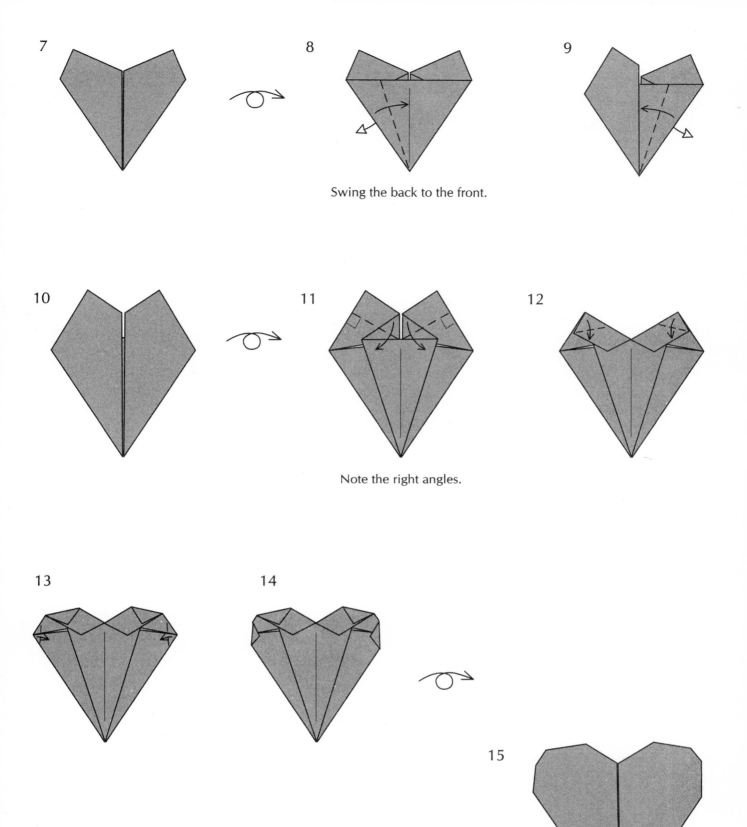

7

8

Swing the back to the front.

9

10

11

Note the right angles.

12

13

14

15

Heart

Boat

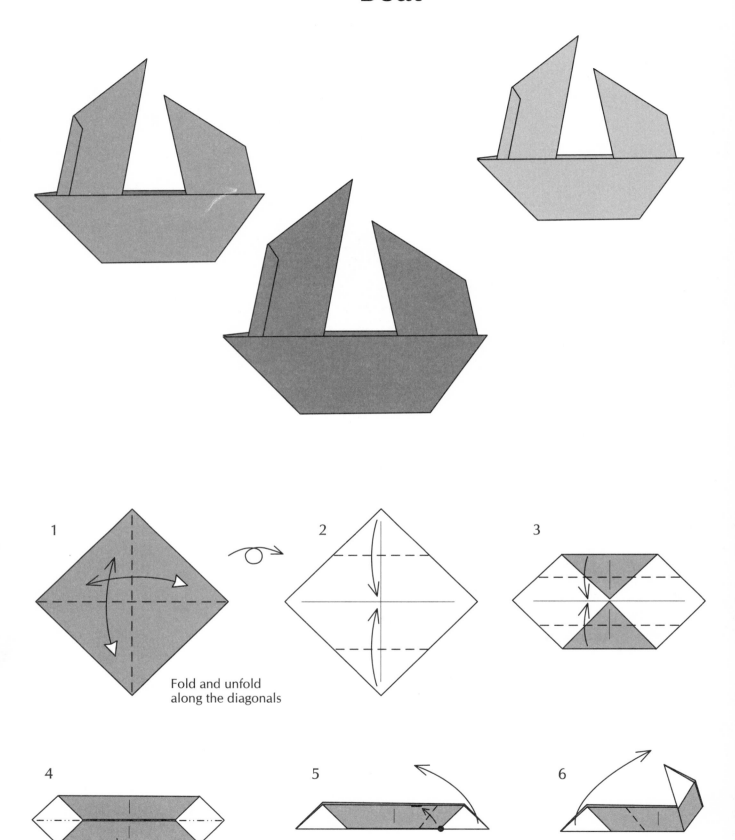

1

Fold and unfold
along the diagonals

2

3

4

5

6

7

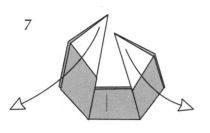

Unfold.

8

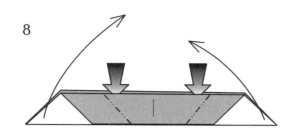

Fold between the layers.

9

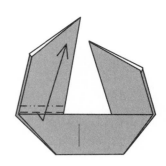

10

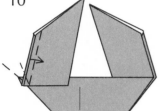

11

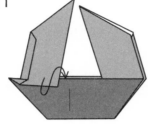

Tuck under the darker paper
(the lower trapezoid).

12

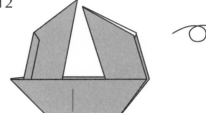

13

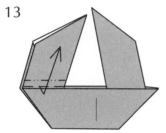

Repeat steps 9–11.

14

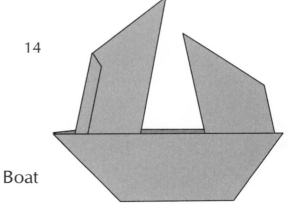

Boat

Twister

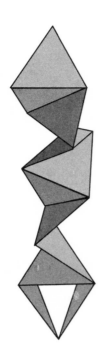

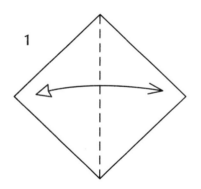

1

Fold and unfold.

2

Fold and unfold.

3

Fold the corners
to the crease.

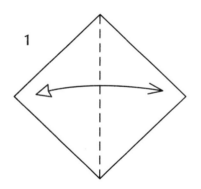

4

5

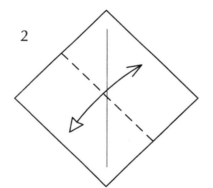

6

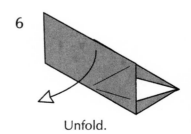

Unfold.

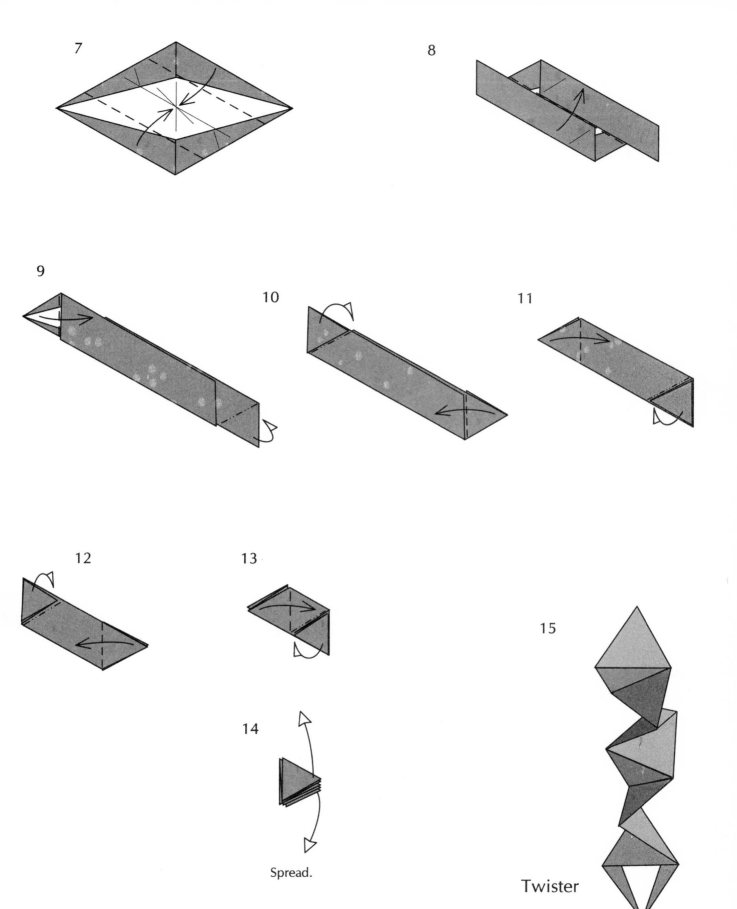

7

8

9

10

11

12

13

14

Spread.

15

Twister

Ornament

1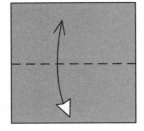

Fold up and unfold.

2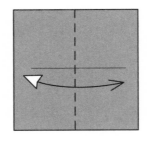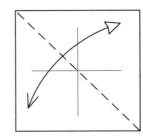

Fold and unfold.

3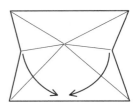

Fold and unfold.

4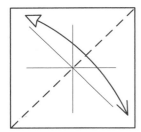

Fold and unfold.

5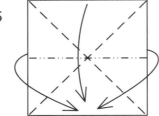

Collapse along the creases.

6

A three-dimensional
intermediate step.

7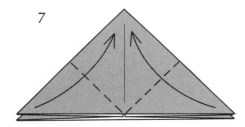

Fold the corners up. Repeat behind.

8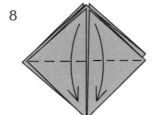

Repeat behind.

Tuck triangle A inside B. The model
will become three-dimensional.
Repeat behind.

9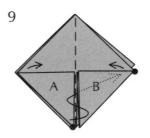

10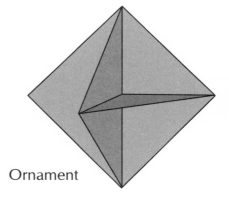

Ornament

3D Diamond

1

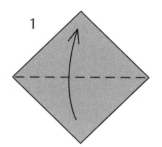

2

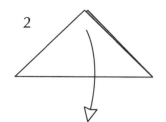

Unfold.

3

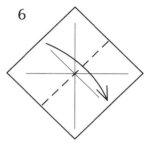

Fold and unfold. Turn over.

4

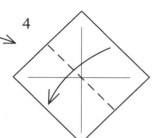

5

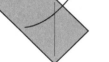

Unfold.

6

Fold in half and rotate.

7

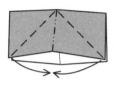

While holding in the air, use the crease lines to bring the lower corners together, then flatten.

8

Repeat behind.

9

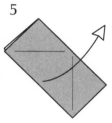

Fold the point down.

10

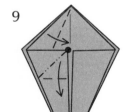

Repeat three more times, on the right and back.

11

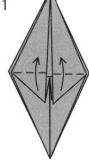

Repeat behind.

12

Tuck triangle A inside B. The model will become three-dimensional. Repeat behind.

13

3D Diamond

Christmas Box

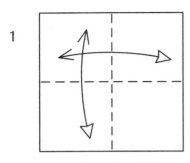

1

Fold and unfold.

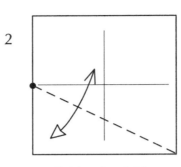

2

Fold and unfold.

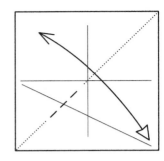

3

Fold and unfold creasing in the lower middle part.

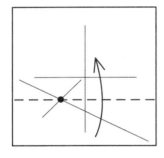

4

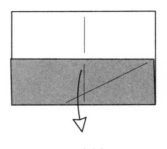

5

Unfold.

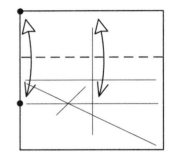

6

Fold and unfold.

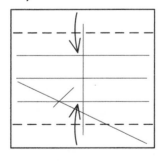

7

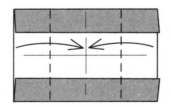

8

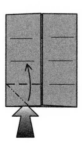

9

Open and spread.

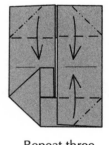

10

Repeat three more times.

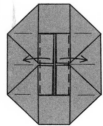

11

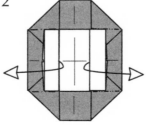

12

Open.

13

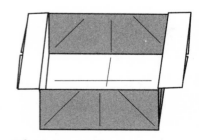

Christmas Box

Gift Box

Designed by Gay Merrill Gross

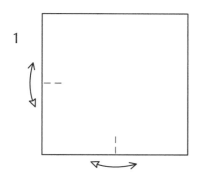

1

Fold and unfold at the edges.

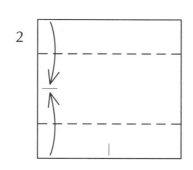

2

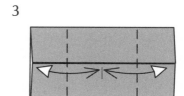

3

Fold to the center and unfold.

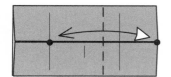

4

Fold and unfold.

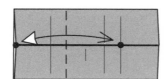

5

Fold and unfold.

6

Fold and unfold
between the creases.

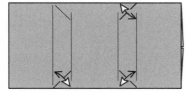

7

Fold and unfold.

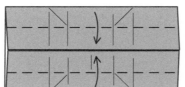

8

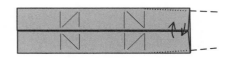

9

Slightly narrow one end. The
middle edges may overlap a little.

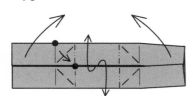

10

Open in the center.

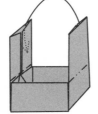

11

Insert one flap into the
other to close the box.

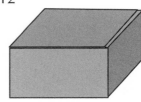

12

Gift Box

3D Tree

Designed by Gay Merrill Gross

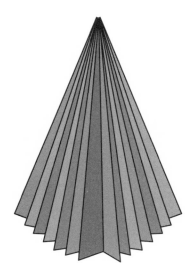

1

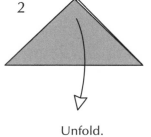

2

Unfold.

3

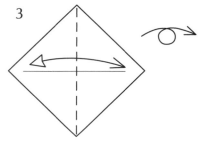

Fold and unfold. Turn over.

4

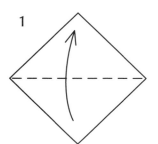

5

Unfold.

6

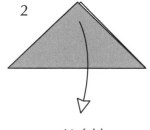

Fold in half and rotate.

7

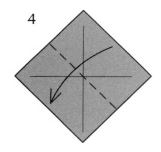

While holding in the air, use the crease lines to bring the lower corners together, then flatten.

8

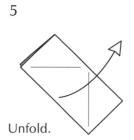

Open and spread. Repeat behind.

9

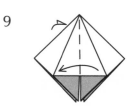

Repeat behind.

10

Open and spread.
Repeat behind.

11

Repeat behind.

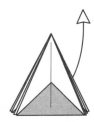

12

Repeat behind.

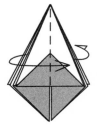

13

Fold two layers.
Repeat behind.

14

Repeat behind.

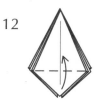

15

Unfold.

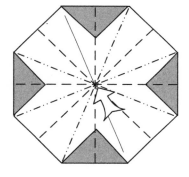

16

Push in at the center and refold.

17

Open and spread.
Repeat behind.

18

Repeat behind.

19

Continue on all eight flaps, taking care to keep
the number of flaps on each side equal. This
balance will help keep the folds accurate.

20

Slightly open the tree at the bottom.
Shape the tree so the flaps are evenly
spaced and stand it up.

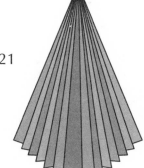

21

3D Tree

Snowman

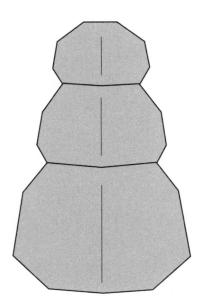

1

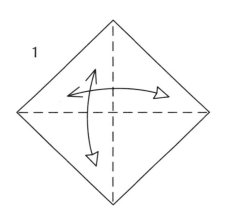

Fold and unfold
along the diagonals.

2

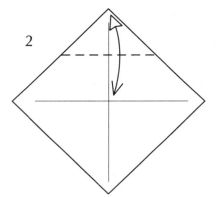

Fold and unfold.

3

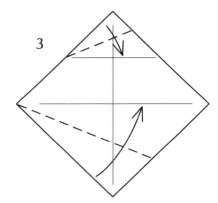

4

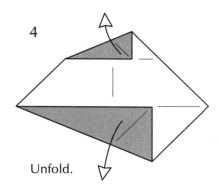

Unfold.

5

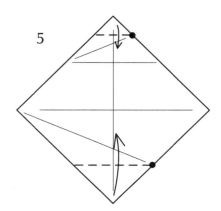

6

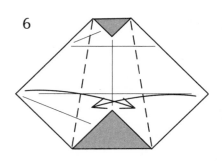

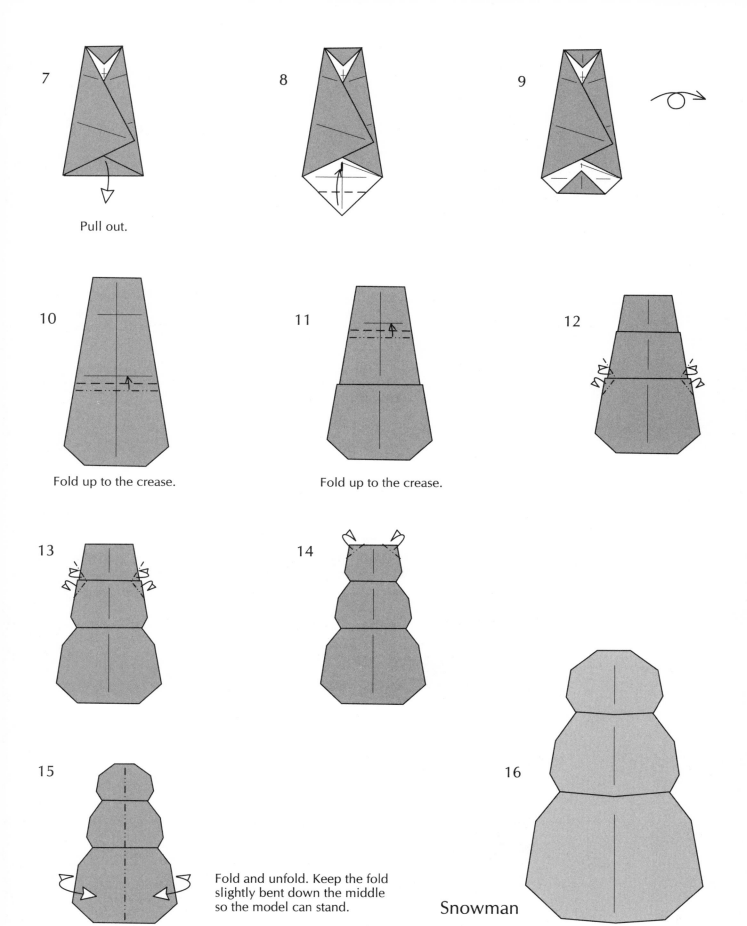

7

Pull out.

8

9

10

Fold up to the crease.

11

Fold up to the crease.

12

13

14

15

Fold and unfold. Keep the fold slightly bent down the middle so the model can stand.

16

Snowman

Angel

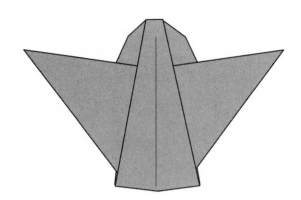

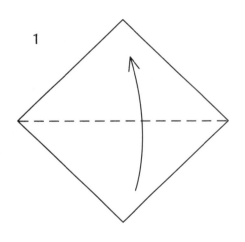
1

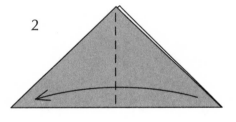
2

3

Repeat behind.

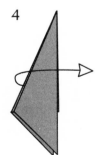
4

Open.

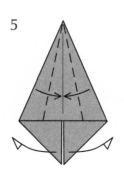
5

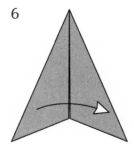
6

Unfold.

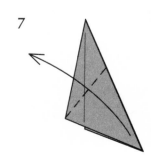
7

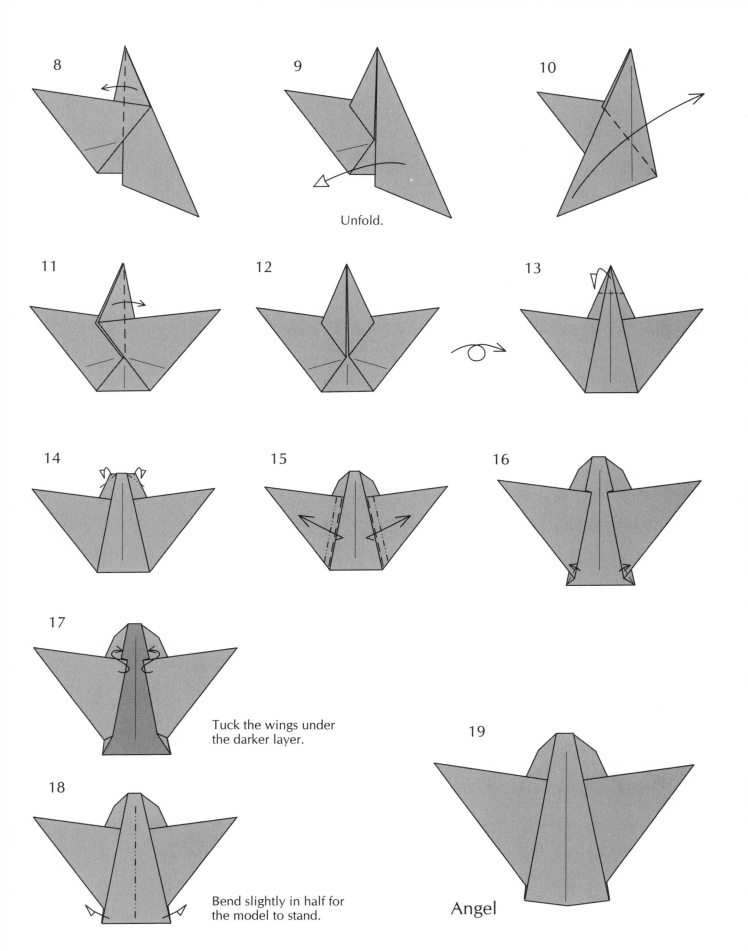

8

9

Unfold.

10

11

12

13

14

15

16

17

Tuck the wings under the darker layer.

18

Bend slightly in half for the model to stand.

19

Angel

Penguin

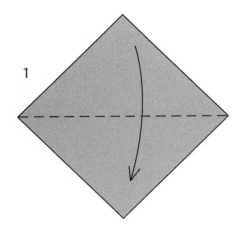

1

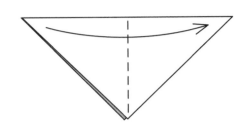

2

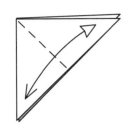

3

Fold and unfold.

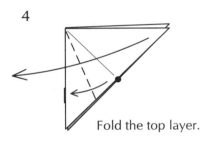

4

Fold the top layer.

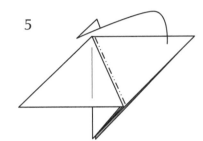

5

6

Pull out the inner layer.

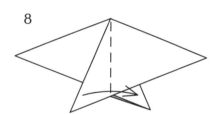

7

Rotate.

8

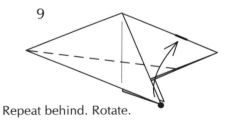

9

Repeat behind. Rotate.

10

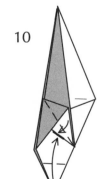

Repeat behind
for the wing.

11

Unfold.

12

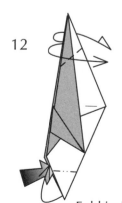

Fold inside at the bottom.
Wrap around at the head.
Adjust the fold at the bottom
so the penguin can stand.

13

Penguin

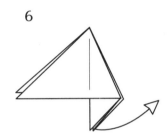

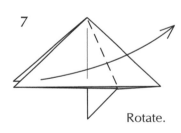

Swan

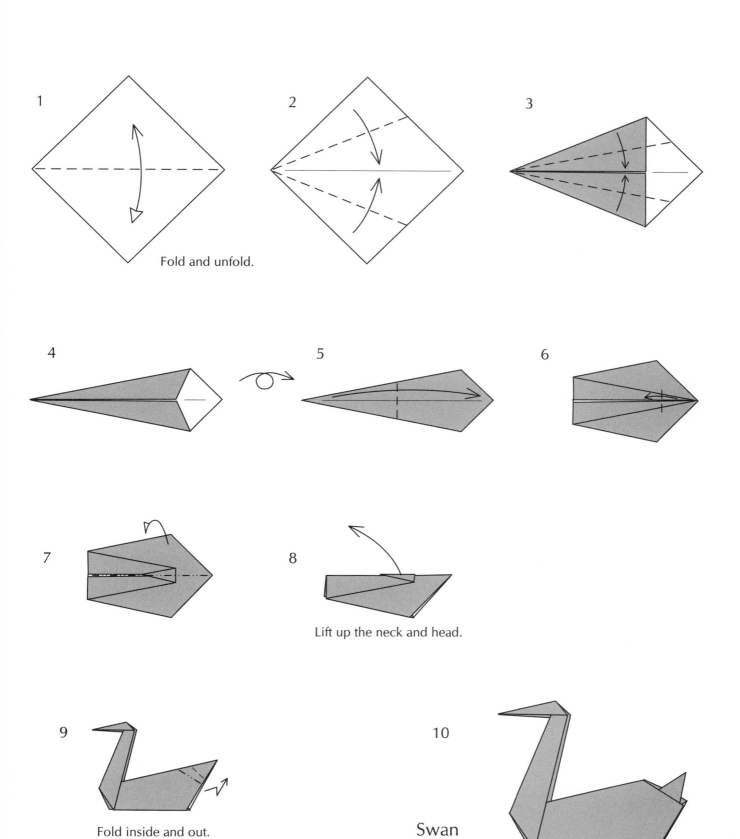

1

Fold and unfold.

2

3

4

5

6

7

8

Lift up the neck and head.

9

Fold inside and out.

10

Swan

Partridge

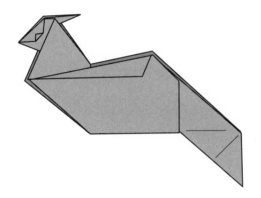

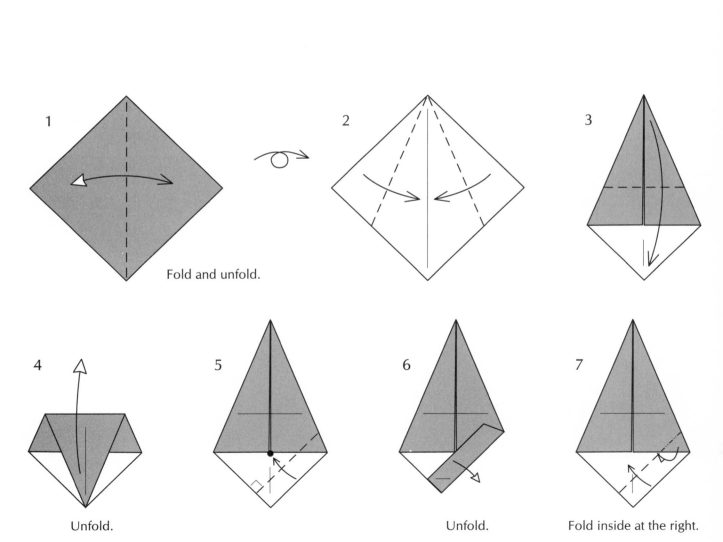

1

Fold and unfold.

2

3

4

Unfold.

5

6

Unfold.

7

Fold inside at the right.

8

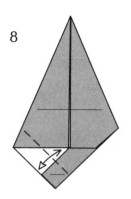

Fold and unfold.

9

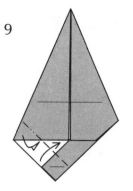

Fold inside at the left.

10

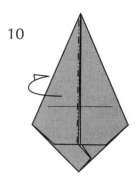

Fold behind and rotate.

11

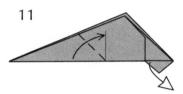

Pull out at the tail and fold to the crease.

12

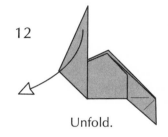

Unfold.

13

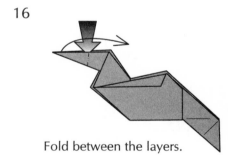

Fold between the layers.

14

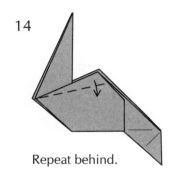

Repeat behind.

15

Fold between the layers.

16

Fold between the layers.

17

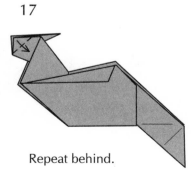

Repeat behind.

18

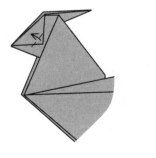

Fold the eye. Repeat behind.

19

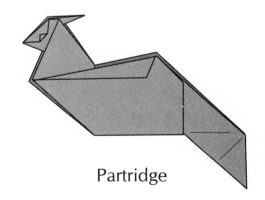

Partridge

Triangular Ornament

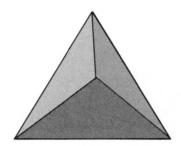

1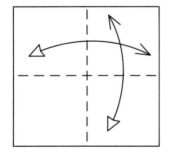

Fold and unfold.

2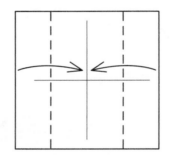

3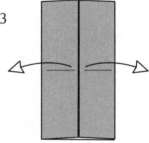

Unfold.

4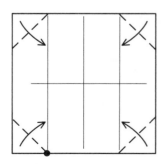

5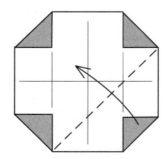

6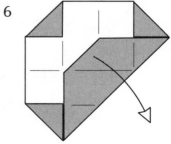

Unfold.

7

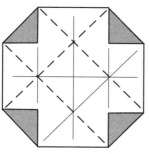

Fold and unfold.

8

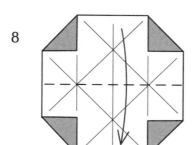

9

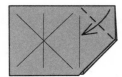

10

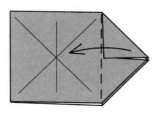

11

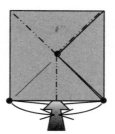

Note the pocket.

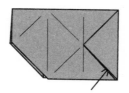

12

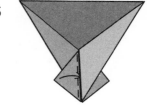

13

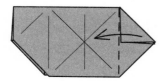

14

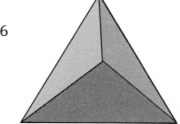

Place your finger inside the model to open it. Bring the lower dots together and puff out at the upper dot.

15

Tuck inside the pocket. Turn over and repeat.

16

Triangular Ornament

Santa Claus

Designed by Linda Mihara

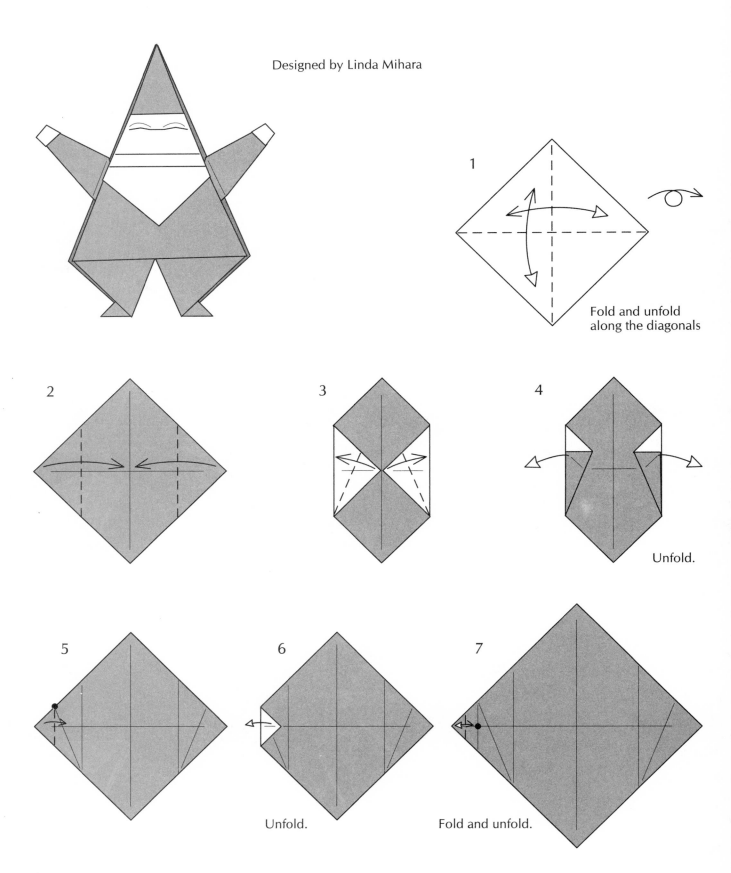

1

Fold and unfold
along the diagonals

2

3

4

Unfold.

5

6

Unfold.

7

Fold and unfold.

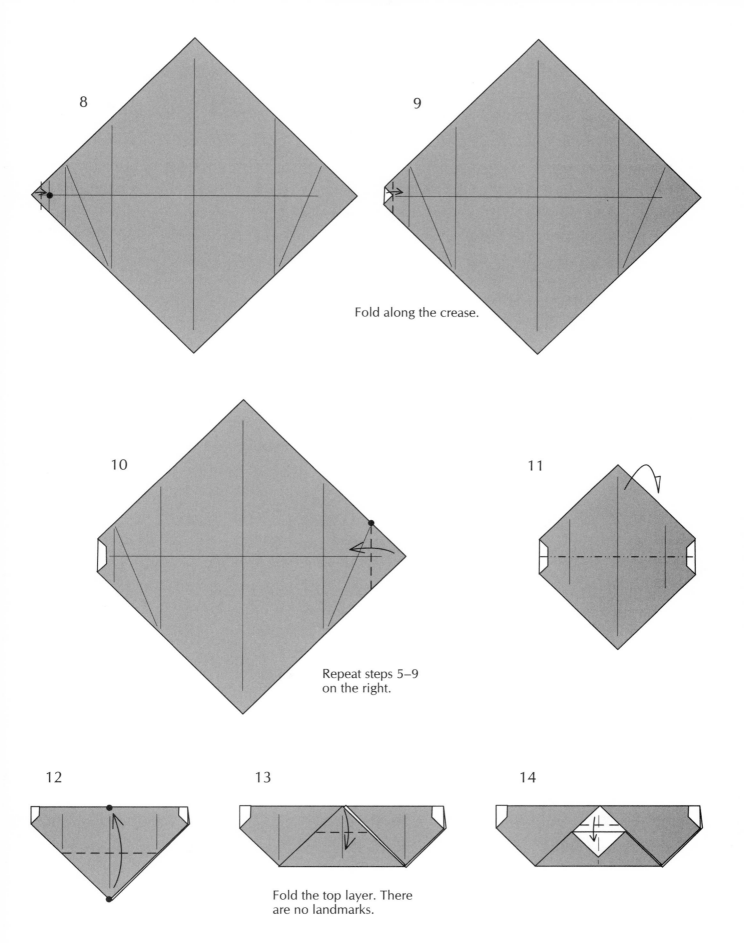

8

9

Fold along the crease.

10

Repeat steps 5–9
on the right.

11

12

13

Fold the top layer. There
are no landmarks.

14

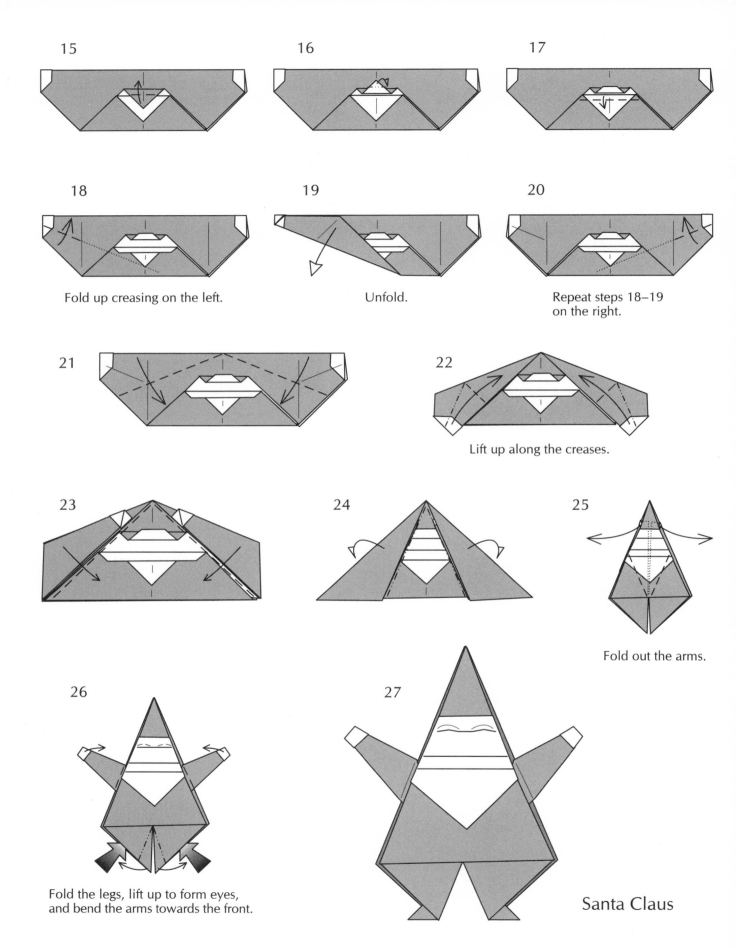

15

16

17

18

Fold up creasing on the left.

19

Unfold.

20

Repeat steps 18–19
on the right.

21

22

Lift up along the creases.

23

24

25

Fold out the arms.

26

Fold the legs, lift up to form eyes,
and bend the arms towards the front.

27

Santa Claus